TAN RABBIT TRAININ[illegible]

Complete Owners [illegible]

The History, Characteristics, Appearance, Breed Standard, Health Issues, Care Requirements, And Much More.

Bright O Erickson

Table of Contents

What This Book Will Teach You

If you want to understand more about rabbits, I highly recommend this Tan Rabbit book. Many subjects pertaining to rabbit farming, care, and behavior are covered.

It offers helpful details about the many varieties and types of rabbits, their behavior, and how to properly care for them, and is presented in simple-to-understand English.

This book begins with an introduction to the many varieties and types of rabbits, along with information on their anatomy and how to recognize them. The article continues by going into great length regarding the various facets of caring for rabbits, such as feeding, housing, medical attention, and grooming.

It also discusses how to avoid and handle issues like gnawing and digging, as well as the many habits of rabbits.

The history of the domestication of rabbits is also covered in this Tan Rabbit book. The various ways that people engage with rabbits and how to protect their health and safety are covered in depth. Also, it includes suggestions on how to cope with negative behaviors like aggressiveness and fear as well as how to bring a new rabbit into the home.

This Tan Rabbit book offers a thorough examination of breeding and reproduction as well as advice on how to choose the ideal breed of rabbit for your residence.

Moreover, it explains how to wean and socialize young rabbits as well as how to care for and prepare for a pregnant rabbit. In general, everyone who wants to understand more about rabbits should definitely read this Tan Rabbit book. It offers a lot of knowledge on everything from choosing the ideal breed to raising a rabbit from birth to old age.

This book is essential reading if you're seeking a complete reference on everything rabbit-related.

CHAPTER ONE

The Introduction Of A Tan Rabbit

The distinctive fur coat of a tan rabbit is a light brown tint, typically with a white undercoat. They are a highly common kind of rabbit and may frequently be found in pet stores. Tan bunnies are highly popular right now because of how calm and kind they are. They are renowned for their wit, devotion, and caring attitudes. A tan rabbit is a fantastic option for anybody searching for a smart, devoted, and devoted companion.

The tan rabbit is a wonderful companion since it has lots of appealing characteristics. They make excellent companions because of their meek and kind temperament. They can be trained to do tricks and obey directions and are also quite intelligent. They are wonderful inside pets and are trainable. Tan rabbits are renowned for their devotion and kind disposition. They like engaging with people since they are very sociable creatures.

Tan rabbits are common in pet stores and make wonderful pets for both kids and adults.

They are quite simple to maintain and take little effort to look after. They may survive for up to eight years or more if given the right care. When purchasing a tan rabbit, it is crucial to do your research on the breed and make sure it receives the right nourishment and activity.

Overall, the tan rabbit is a superb pet option for anyone searching for a wise, devoted, and devoted friend. They are sociable and are capable of developing close relationships with their owners.

They may make fantastic lifetime companions if given the right care and diet.

A Tan Rabbit's Origin And History

The domestic rabbit breed known as the Tan, or simply Tan, got its start in Scotland in the late 19th century.

The breed, notable for its unusual coloring, was produced by mating a Belgian Hare with a Dutch Rabbit.

Tan rabbits have a light tan coat that can range in hue from sand to dark chocolate.

The breed features a pointed face, tiny ears, and a lean physique.

One of the oldest breeds of rabbits, the Tan has a long history in Scotland. The late 1800s saw the development of this breed, which was selected for its even coat and friendly disposition.

One of the first breeds to be displayed at dog shows, tans received their own breed standard in the early 1900s. Tan rabbits are a well-liked breed that is highly regarded by both pet owners and breeders.

For those searching for a more compact, devoted companion, it’s even coat of hair and amiable disposition make it the perfect option.

The breed can adapt to a wide range of environments and temperatures and is also comparatively resilient. Tan rabbits are a popular species, although they can be challenging to produce. As the bunnies are notorious for being little, it may be challenging to keep them at the ideal size and coat quality.

While the rabbits may generate a broad range of hues from

sandy to rich chocolate tones, breeding for the right color might be difficult.

The Tan rabbit is one of the oldest breeds of domestic rabbits and continues to be a popular breed despite these difficulties. It is the perfect pet due to its even coat, pleasant temperament, and durability.

It is also a fantastic alternative for individuals searching for a smaller, more cuddly companion.

The Tan kind of rabbit is one that will make any home happy.

Characteristics Of A Tan Rabbit

A breed of rabbit with a special and unusual appearance is the tan rabbit. Their short to medium-length coats can contain tan fur that ranges in hue from pale to dark brown. They have a long, thin body type and round, floppy ears.

Tan rabbits are excellent pets since they are sociable and extroverted. They like playing and exploring their environment, and they are also quite energetic. Tan rabbits live up to 10 years or more and are often in good condition. Its fur can range in color from white to brown, and it can weigh between 2 and 8 pounds. Tan bunnies are renowned for their wit and vivacity as well. They make great companions and are readily taught.

Tan rabbits are often simple to care for and are adept at adjusting to their surroundings. They need routine grooming and a diet high in fresh produce. Tan rabbits like running, leaping, and exploring, and they also require a lot of exercises.

Tan rabbits are an excellent breed that is sociable, perceptive, and simple to care for. They make wonderful friends and may give years of love and company.

CHAPTER TWO

Appearance Of A Tan Rabbit

A breed of rabbit with a special, recognizable appearance is the tan rabbit. Its fur has a creamy golden shade with perhaps faint reddish or brown undertones. The rabbit looks particularly fluffy and silky since its hair is often short and thick.

The ears are huge and erect, and the eyes are often a rich, dark brown. The rabbit has a spherical, compact body, short, powerful legs, and a short, fluffy tail.

The tan bunny is highly animated and enjoys playing and adventuring. It is a perceptive breed that is frequently spotted digging and investigating its surroundings. This breed enjoys being around other animals and humans and is also quite sociable.

It is well recognized for being extremely loving and cuddly, and it frequently seeks human attention for cuddling and caressing. The brown rabbit is the perfect pet for anybody searching for a fun and energetic friend.

It's a great choice for families with kids because of its kind disposition and loving behavior. It is a fantastic option for anyone who wants a pet that is simple to train and care for. Although having certain health difficulties, the tan rabbit breed is generally considered to be in good condition.

They comprise eye issues, dental issues, and ear infections. The easiest method to avoid these problems is to maintain a clean environment for the rabbit and to provide it a nutritious food.

The Tan rabbit is an attractive and endearing breed all around. With its unique appearance and kind nature, it would make a great pet for any family. The tan rabbit may make a delightful companion for many years if given the right care and attention.

Breed Specifications For A Tan Rabbit

A medium-sized breed with many different color variations is the tan rabbit. The breed, which is currently the most well-known among American breeds, was initially acknowledged in the country in 1942.

The Tan Rabbit weighs around 4-5 pounds on average, making it a medium-sized breed. The head is small and wide, and the body is compact and well-muscled with a big, rounded chest.

The ears are half-lopped and have a little upper arch. The thick, velvety fur is available in a range of hues, including lilac, blue, chocolate, and black.

The fur must be uniform in length and texture, free of any spots or discolorations, and conform to the breed standard.

The hue and tones of the fur should be consistent throughout. The ears should be large, uniform in length, and devoid of knots.

The nose should be clearly defined, and the eyes should be bright and distinct. The Tan Rabbit is renowned for being a very gregarious and sociable breed, and they make wonderful companions. They are also renowned for being low-maintenance because of their little grooming needs and simplicity of upkeep.

The Tan Rabbit is a fantastic option for both novice and

seasoned rabbit keepers. They are a resilient breed that is able to function in both indoor and outdoor environments. They are an excellent choice for families or first-time bunny owners because they are also quite simple to train.

Overall, the Tan Rabbit is a lovely breed that requires little care. They are an excellent choice for both inexperienced and seasoned rabbit owners and make lovely companions. They are certain to offer delight to any home thanks to their vast range of colors and even temperaments.

Issues With A Tan Rabbit's Health

For many individuals, a tan rabbit makes an appealing and well-liked pet. They can, however, experience some health problems, just like any other animal, and their owners should be aware of these. Dental issues are one of the most often reported difficulties with Tan rabbits. These animals require routine dental examinations and, if necessary, tooth trimming since their teeth continue to develop throughout their lives.

Tan rabbits' teeth are particularly vulnerable since they are smaller than those of other breeds. Dental issues left untreated might result in poor nutrition and infection.

Obesity is another problem that is frequently observed in tan rabbits. These bunnies are prone to overeating, which causes weight gain, much like other animals.

Tan rabbit owners should be sure to provide them a balanced, healthy food and lots of exercises to maintain a healthy weight. Tan rabbits are susceptible to parasite issues as well. As opposed to other breeds, these animals are more prone to fleas, mites, and other parasites, thus frequent grooming and flea treatment are crucial.

Lastly, respiratory infections can also be a problem for tan rabbits. Because these creatures might be particularly sensitive to variations in temperature and humidity, it's crucial to maintain a pleasant habitat for them.

It's crucial to take your Tan rabbit to the vet for treatment if they exhibit any symptoms of a respiratory illness, like discharge from the nose or eyes, coughing, or sneezing. Tan rabbit owners may make sure that their pets remain content and healthy by taking the appropriate precautions to avoid and cure these health problems. Each pet, even the Tan rabbit, needs regular veterinary appointments, adequate grooming, and balanced food to be healthy.

Treatment And Prevention For Tan Rabbits

Tan rabbits are a popular breed that can be found in households all around the world and make a wonderful addition to any family. Nonetheless, it is crucial to understand how to avoid and handle any health problems that might develop with this kind of rabbit.

The most crucial action to do to prevent health problems in Tan rabbits is to give them a tidy and cozy habitat. Make sure your rabbit isn't exposed to other animals, and that the cage is maintained tidy.

In addition, make sure the rabbit is eating well and getting enough activity. They will remain robust and healthy as a result of this.

Take your Tan rabbit to the veterinarian as soon as you notice any symptoms of the disease.

Ear mites, respiratory diseases, hair loss, and skin infections are typical conditions that Tan rabbits can suffer from. The severity of the symptoms and the underlying cause of these diseases will determine the course of treatment.

It's crucial to frequently groom your Tan rabbit in addition to taking it to the doctor on a regular basis. By doing this, you can maintain the fur tidy and clear of trash and parasites.

To help keep your rabbit healthy, remember to frequently wash their teeth and trim their nails. Finally, it's critical to keep an eye out for any modifications in behavior or health in your Tan rabbit. Take your rabbit to the doctor straight away if you find that they are getting sluggish, losing its appetite, or having trouble breathing. You can assist your Tan rabbit avoid and treat any health problems by following these instructions.

CHAPTER THREE

Care Requirements For A Tan Rabbit

Tan rabbits have a few care needs that, if satisfied, will maintain your pet's health. They require, like other rabbits, a roomy, expansive habitat with room to hop, leap, and explore. To keep them occupied, their cage should also have a lot of hay and a selection of chew toys.

Tan rabbits should also always have access to plenty of fresh water as well as a range of fresh fruits and vegetables.

In order to maintain the health of their digestive systems, they need also to receive hay daily. Tan rabbits should have their fur combed frequently to maintain it lustrous and free of matting when it comes to maintenance. Regular nail trimming is also necessary to keep them safe from injuries and infections.

Tan rabbits should often be taken outside of their enclosure for exercise so they may stretch their legs and investigate. Either an enclosed, secure outdoor space or a secure inside space can be used for this.

Lastly, tan bunnies should receive a lot of affection and care. Being sociable creatures, rabbits require interaction with their owners.

To establish a relationship and keep your rabbit healthy and content, spend time caressing and playing with them each day. Your Tan rabbit will grow and make a delightful companion if you adhere to these easy maintenance instructions.

Training

An enjoyable experience can come from training a tan rabbit. It's critical to realize that rabbits are clever creatures who can be educated with time, persistence, and praise.

Creating a secure and cozy home is the first step in teaching a tan rabbit. In addition to giving the rabbit enough food, drink, and shelter, this entails making sure it has enough room to wander and explore.

When the setting has been created, it is crucial to start the training procedure. Positive reinforcement is the best method for training a tan rabbit. This includes rewarding positive actions with sweets, verbal compliments, and affection. It's crucial to use incentives consistently and to only acknowledge desired behavior. Also, it's critical to ignore undesirable actions in order to teach the bunny that they are not desired. It's crucial to set and adhere to a schedule for the rabbit. The rabbit will get a better understanding of expectations thanks to this. Also, it's critical to make sure the rabbit gets lots of social contact and exercise because these factors will improve their general well-being.

If done correctly, training a tan rabbit might end up being a great time. It's crucial to exercise patience, consistency, and positive reinforcement.

It's crucial to establish a routine for the rabbit and to provide a secure and pleasant environment for it. Tan rabbits are trainable and can be trained to behave nicely and make good pets.

Exercise

Tan rabbit exercise may be enjoyable and gratifying for you and your fuzzy pet. The right quantity of exercise must be provided to all rabbits each day in order to ensure their overall health and welfare.

Allowing your tan rabbit to hop and run around the house without restraint is the greatest method to exercise. This provides them an opportunity to explore, get some much-needed exercise, and stretch their legs. As they are natural explorers, rabbits will enjoy exploring various rooms in your house. If at all feasible, give them a ton of playthings and barriers to investigating. You may also take your rabbit for a leisurely walk outside if you don't have enough room inside for them to run about unrestrainedly. They will be able to explore the outdoors, get some sunshine and fresh air, and expend some of their surplus energy.

Always keep an eye on them, and if necessary, keep them on a leash. Ultimately, you may construct a playground for bunnies inside. The toys kids can use to explore and exercise include tunnels, homes, and other objects. This is a fantastic method to keep kids occupied and encourage movement, which is important for their mental and physical health.

Tan rabbits need exercise for their health and happiness, and it's also a terrific way to strengthen your relationship with your pet. They should have lots of opportunities to wander about and investigate, and you should always keep an eye on them. Exercise time can be made enjoyable and rewarding for both you and your furry pet with a little bit of work and imagination.

Grooming

Owning a Tan rabbit requires careful grooming. Tan rabbits have a smooth, glossy coat that has to be brushed and cared for on a regular basis to keep them looking beautiful.

Use a slicker brush to groom your Tan rabbit for the finest results. The coat will be cleaned of any dirt, debris, and knots with this brush.

Be careful to brush the belly, tail, and legs as well as the entire coat. Together with combing, it's crucial to keep your Tan rabbit's claws well-trimmed. Every two to three weeks, this should be done with a pair of nail clippers. Be careful to avoid clipping the quick, the pink region in the center of the nail that houses the blood vessels, and just the nail tips. Bathing Tan rabbits every few months is a crucial component of grooming them. Make use of a moderate pet-safe soap that has been diluted in warm water. Be sure to thoroughly rinse off the soap before using a towel to pat the rabbit dry.

Lastly, it's crucial to often examine the eyes and ears of your Tan rabbit. Clean the ears and eyes with a wet cloth, making sure to get rid of any dirt or debris.

Take your Tan rabbit to the vet for an accurate diagnosis and treatment if they exhibit any indications of infection.

Regular grooming is necessary to maintain your Tan rabbit healthy and attractive. Your Tan rabbit may look and feel its best with routine brushing, nail clipping, baths, and ear and eye cleaning.

Socialization

The socialization of a Tan rabbit plays a crucial role in its growth. A rabbit is taught to trust and respond to people through socialization, which also teaches it to feel secure and at ease in its surroundings.

Your rabbit will become a confident and sociable companion if you socialize them properly.

Providing a Tan rabbit with a secure habitat is the first step in socializing it. This entails giving it a cage with plenty of hiding spots and enough room for it to wander around and investigate. There should be a variety of things in the hiding spots, such as boxes, logs, and tunnels. This will provide the rabbit with a safe haven to retire to in times of danger or stress.

The next phase is to begin exposing the Tan rabbit to

people when the setting has been established. Just place yourself close to the rabbit and start talking to it calmly. Give the rabbit snacks and gradually get closer to it over time. When the rabbit is ready, let it come up to you.

Getting a Tan rabbit accustomed to being handled is an essential component in socializing them. Start by softly petting its fur, then go toward lifting it up. If the rabbit starts to feel uncomfortable, stop and let it settle before continuing.

Always go carefully and avoid pressuring the rabbit into doing anything it doesn't want to do. Lastly, it's critical to provide the Tan rabbit with a lot of opportunities for play. Because they are social creatures, rabbits require the ability to communicate with both people and other rabbits.

To keep the rabbit interested and occupied, provide a variety of toys and interactive games. The process of socializing with a Tan rabbit is crucial and fruitful. You may assist your rabbit in becoming a self-assured and sociable pet by being consistent and patient with it.

Housing

According to the size and demands of the rabbit, several types of housing are needed for Tan Rabbits. A cage for a little rabbit has to be at least 2 feet wide, 2 feet deep, and 2 feet high. The rabbit should be able to play and roam freely because of this. For the rabbit's safety from harm and escape, the cage should also have a sturdy bottom and sides.

To keep the rabbit safe from predators, the cage should also include a door that is locked or latches securely.

The habitat should include plenty of space for the rabbit to play and explore as well as room to bounce around and extend their legs.

A bigger rabbit might need to live in an outside hutch or shed. This needs to be built of a durable material with good ventilation, such as metal or wood.

The hutch should be constructed to be waterproof and have a safe entrance to keep predators away. The rabbit should have plenty of space in the hutch to play, exercise, and investigate. A litter box or tray should also be included in the housing, along with a lot of hay, straw, or shredded paper for the rabbit to cuddle in. In order to maintain a good set of teeth, the rabbit should also have access to a variety of toys and other objects to gnaw on.

To avoid the rabbit getting sick, the housing must also be maintained dry and clean. Regular maintenance should include cleaning the cage at least once a week and inspecting it for signs of wear or damage. The Tan Rabbit may live a long and healthy life if the proper home is provided.

CHAPTER FOUR

Needs For A Tan Rabbit's Diet

A Tan rabbit is a rare breed of rabbit distinguished by its characteristic tan hue and particular nutritional needs.

The Tan rabbit has a special diet that is distinct from that of other rabbit breeds.

In comparison to other breeds, it requires more protein and requires more than just hay, fruits, and vegetables to be healthy. The Tan rabbit requires several types of fresh, premium hay as well as grasses like timothy and orchard grass. It also requires a range of fresh fruits and vegetables, such as celery, apples, and carrots. The Tan rabbit furthermore needs premium pellets created especially for this species.

The Tan rabbit also needs constant access to clean water. It is crucial to supply fresh, clean water on a regular basis and to replace the water often. To keep the Tan rabbit interested and active, it's essential to give it a variety of toys and snacks. No processed food or food with a lot of sugar or fat should be provided to the

Tan rabbit. They may be harmful to the Tan rabbit and cause weight gain as well as other health issues.

Also, it's crucial to keep the Tan rabbit's treatment intake in check because too many treats might contribute to obesity. Lastly, it's critical to provide the Tan rabbit with a nutritious food that is both varied and balanced. Fresh hay, grasses, produce, fruits, and high-quality pellets should all be part of this diet. Make sure the Tan rabbit has access to clean water, as well as a selection of toys and treats.

The Tan rabbit's health and welfare depend on you eating according to these rules.

Choosing A Partner

A Tan rabbit's mate choosing is a significant choice that has to be carefully considered. It is crucial to take into account the rabbit's genetic makeup, overall health, and compatibility with the other rabbit.

Genetics must be taken into account while choosing a Tan rabbit's mate. Depending on their genetic composition, tan rabbits can have various hues of tan.

Tan rabbits come in a variety of tones, including light, golden, and even dark brown. To increase your chances of having healthy babies, choose a mate who is also a comparable shade of tan.

Also, the rabbit's well-being needs to be taken into account. The best odds of having healthy kids depend on choosing a spouse who is in good health. It's also crucial to make sure the two rabbits get along and are compatible with one another. It's crucial to choose a partner whom the Tan rabbit feels at ease with because rabbits may be finicky about their partners. The size of the rabbit should also be taken into account when choosing a partner.

It's critical to choose a mate that is compatible in size because rabbit breeds might differ in size. This will guarantee that the rabbits can reproduce and have healthy young.

In conclusion, picking a mate for a Tan rabbit is a choice that should be carefully considered. When choosing a partner, it's critical to take genetics, health, and compatibility into account. The size of the rabbit should also be taken into account while choosing a partner in order to guarantee that the rabbits can successfully mate and have healthy progeny.

Reproduction

Tan rabbits can reproduce naturally or artificially, and both methods are quite simple. Tan rabbits normally give birth in the spring and early summer in the wild. Breeding couples of rabbits will build a den during this period and mate there.

Tan rabbit litters typically include 4–7 kits, however, up to 10-kit litters have also been seen.

Tan rabbits are frequently produced for exhibition and as pets by artificial reproduction, which is also a possibility. Without any physical touch, two rabbits can mate through artificial insemination. This method is frequently applied to improve the likelihood of producing Tan rabbits of show quality.

Tan rabbits typically go through a gestation period of 31 days. Kits typically weigh less than 1/4 pound when they are born. Their coat will continue to take on a characteristic golden brown hue as they mature, which usually takes approximately 8 months.

Tan rabbits may be kept either indoors or outside, although as house pets, they are usually kept inside. Tan rabbits are often home pets maintained in cages or hutches with lots of space to roam and explore.

Tan rabbits may be housed outside, but they must be protected from predators and the environment. To sum up, the Tan rabbit is a rare variety of domesticated rabbits that is distinguished by its peculiar hair and coloring.

Tan rabbits can reproduce naturally or artificially, and both methods are quite simple.

Tan rabbits are often home pets maintained in cages or hutches with lots of space to roam and explore.

CHAPTER FIVE

How To Get A Tan Rabbit Ready For A Show And The Value Of Presentation

The presentation is the most crucial aspect to take into account while getting a Tan rabbit ready for a show. The Tan rabbit must be presented well in order to appear at its finest and be judge-ready.

The rabbit should first receive thorough grooming. This involves detangling any mats, cutting the nails, cleaning the ears, and performing any other essential upkeep.

Also, it's crucial to keep the rabbit's fur clean and clear of dirt and debris. The best way to maintain the appearance of the fur is with regular brushing or combing. The rabbit must then be outfitted for the performance in the following phase. This involves choosing the appropriate clothing and ensuring the rabbit can comfortably wear it. Typically, a show dress consists of a white shirt, tan slacks or a skirt, and a bow tie.

The outfit should be designed to fit the rabbit's body, be clear of stains, and have no rips.

It's crucial to display the Tan rabbit in its best light before the performance.

Taking care of the rabbit's nutrition and hydration is a part of this. The rabbit may look sleepy and uninterested in competing if it is malnourished. The rabbit should also have plenty of time to adjust to its new surroundings. When the rabbit is submitted for judgment, this will enable it to be less anxious and more peaceful.

Finally, it's critical to keep in mind that a good event relies heavily on presentation.

This involves ensuring the bunny is well-groomed and has a cheerful attitude. The rabbit's clothes should also be well-fitting and devoid of any stains or rips. The Tan rabbit will look its finest and be prepared to perform in the show thanks to all of these things.

Advantages Of Keeping A Tan Rabbit

An enjoyable experience can come from having a tan rabbit. Owning a tan rabbit has several advantages, from their endearing personalities to their simple maintenance requirements. Tan rabbits are renowned for having a patient, kind nature, which makes them the perfect companion for households with young children. They like engaging with people and are also quite sociable.

Tan rabbits are quite simple to care for and simply require routine daily upkeep. They may easily be kept in tiny living spaces because they don't need a lot of room. Moreover, they don't need much grooming, and their coats require little upkeep. Tan rabbits are reasonably inexpensive pets since they have limited food requirements and little need for medical care. Tan rabbits may live up to 10 years if given the correct care, giving their owners a lot of time together. They are also extremely clever, which makes them simple to teach and provides a ton of entertainment options.

Tan rabbits require a lot of exercise and activity since they are highly energetic. Last but not least, tan rabbits are a fantastic tool to teach kids responsibility.

Children can learn responsibility and empathy by taking care of a pet. While they are in charge of caring for their pet, it may also teach them how to take care of themselves.

Overall, having a tan rabbit may be highly profitable and pleasurable. They not only make excellent friends, but they also offer many chances to teach kids valuable life lessons.

Conclusion

The adorable tan rabbit may provide happiness and companionship to any home. It is a devoted pet that enjoys receiving attention. It is simple to take care of and simple to train.

Anybody seeking a smaller pet should choose a tan rabbit.

Tan rabbits are still fairly energetic and like to play, even if they might not be as active as some other breeds. They like to interact with people and spend time with their owners. They need consistent physical activity, a balanced diet, and frequent grooming.

Overall, the Tan Rabbit makes a wonderful companion. They can fit into any family and are devoted and affectionate. They are simple to take care of and make wonderful pets for tiny spaces.

Printed in Great Britain
by Amazon

23280182R00040